Right now, the pages that you hold are turning ever onward. A lot has happened to me. And there are still a lot of things that I wouldn't let myself say in the last book that are affecting me daily. It is hard to put it all behind me.

My first chapbook, **Random Acts of Verse,** was a moderate success. And I am eternally grateful for the support and opportunities that writing that book has given me.

While plotting the pages for **My Revolution**, I decided to include some examples of prose with my poetry. I think that is fair, don't you? I mean, I could tell you my continuing life's story, or I could show it to you in prose and verse.

I think you would prefer the latter. So, I will save any explanations I may have for the end.

Thank you for reading this far and I sincerely hope you enjoy my revolution.

Please Enjoy!

MY REVOLUTION

Jacqueline Nicole Harris

Thanks for your support! And keep writing and reciting your own.

— Jacqueline N. Harris

Cover design by
Marques Smith-Walker

I.G.S Promotions & Ent.
igspromoent@gmail.com

HE LOVED ME

BROKEN PIECES

A REGRET

DELICATE

WE

THIRSTY

RAGE OF BLACKNESS

MY REVOLUTION

COMMON

THE FINGER

THE RULES FOR GOING H.A.M.

MY SOUND

THE REASON

PLAYING PROMETHEUS

WAITING

THESE HANDS

THANK GOD FOR WHO I AM NOT

DOWN

REFLECTING IN THE LIGHT OF MO'BETTA BLUES

THE BLUES FALLS LIKE RAIN FOR ME

WHEN TAALAM KISSED THE APPLES OF MY CHEEKS

HE LOVED ME

He loved me.
And for a time it was good.
Sucking and savoring salt and sweat—
Sealing our doom with shallow promises and kisses.
He loved me, I think.
Only much to my chagrin,
I took him in again and again.
Like a lost runaway puppy
whose wandering affections would chafe
my inner thighs, I took him all in,
the good and the bad of it.
I had been waiting for it.
I thought this is what is expected
of lovers in love. I thought.
But, what did I really know?
He only loved me,
used me,
knew me,
corrupted and broke me.
And, silly me,
I hardly recognized myself
without his caresses and lies.
He was everything and
our time meant nothing.
But, it is only right for me
to acknowledge now,
that I loved him back.

BROKEN PIECES

I keep dancing
on a lot
of broken pieces.
Thin skinned,
the bitter regrets
of my past pierce
through to my soul.
Crawling on my belly
like a worm,
the acrid smell
of past mistakes
and defeats
wafts in my nostrils.

I think I've been
to this party before.

This constant,
never ending dance
is affectionately nicknamed
bipolar mania
by those who are
too educated to know
any better.

But I don't need
their insight
to know what this is.

This is Hell.

Will someone please
help me find a way out
or at least change that record
we are spinning on called Earth?
I can't stand this
same sorry song,
this malodorous melody,
this existence fucking sucks.

Especially when
someone taps me
on my right shoulder
and asks me to dance
by saying,
why don't you just smile,
and/or my personal favorite,
everything is going to be ok.

And I dance.
Or at least I try
to find the beat
that will make me
fit into the groove,
make me hip to the jive,
make me not a wallflower
in my own life.
I dance.

While inwardly

I want to vomit
in my hand
and throw it in the
face of the world.
Because it is all
the same song
and dance shit to me daily—
just a different tempo.

I feel like
a robot monkey,
standing stagnant
in my own tight shoes,
and it's not ok
and I don't think smiling
is going to fix it.
Not This. Not Me.

And then someone taps me
on my left shoulder and says:
Well, you're just being morbid,
negative, and obtuse.
You're going to bring
everybody down.
And then finally I say:
Well,
I don't think
your comfort level
should hinge
so precariously
on my mood,

and if you
tap me again,
I'm going to bite
your fucking finger
off.

Yes.

It is that
kind of behavior
that has made me
captive in my own
skin.

Who's behavior?
Yours and mine.

I shouldn't be drowning
in fresh air, but I am.
And it's not my fault.
And it's not your fault.

So, stop trying
to use words
to define something
you don't understand.
Don't try to fix me.
I have to live through this.
Alone.

And when I'm ready
for a dance partner,
I'll call.

A REGRET

We did it
like two long lost lovers,
trysting in the shadows for salvation
with absolutely nothing
between us but our flesh,
our bones and the pace of our
rhythmically panting breaths.

And when it was over,
a day later,
I felt like it was the dumbest
thing I had ever done.

Why?

Well, I was understandably needy.
Denying myself so long the pleasures
of wanton abandon,
had left me sated in bitterness.
Also, when I am needy,
I have the IQ of a rock.

So, I can't knock him
for being a typical man
when I, myself,
should have been more
than a typical woman.

I should have been more than that.
We could have been more than that.

But,

at the end
of the night,
it was just a tryst.

A rhythmic,
energizing tryst
that gushed
like a river
down the drain.

Both of us
grasping feverishly
at a moment
that was nothing
but sex and wasted time.

We could have made deeper memories.
I can see that now.
I could have told him my favorite color.
He could have told me his favorite food.
I could have made that for him.

That would have been easier than making love.
Such a silly statement that is---*making love*.
I don't think love is something you make.
I don't know how to make love.

All I have right now
is this shallow grave
in my mind which shells inside of it
the reanimated corpse of a broken dream;
a constant reminder that good girls
can't play bad without consequence.

The corpse reminds me of my actions
on that particular midnight.
It says,
no matter where you go girl
there you are.
Alone.
Now grow the fuck up
and deal with it girl.
Grow up and deal with it.

DELICATE

I have wanted to say this
since I met you.
Say it and not shout it
from the hillside just hoping
you can catch the sound.
This is not for the world to hear.

This has been
weighing on my
heart for a long time
and what I have to say to
you is delicate.
I want to whisper
this in your ear, softly.
Let it float into your subconscious,
mingle with your desires,
placate your every thought,
and shatter any doubts in your mind.
I want you.

My life is complicated,
as is yours,
and honestly
I can't tell the difference
from the night and the morning.

Daily, I wonder where you are,
what and how you are doing.
And nightly?

Nightly, I find myself
yearning for you, beside me

while the hunger for the taste
of your skin wets my lips.

I can barely contain
the fathomless emotions radiating
from the core of my being as I imagine
your hands grabbing me,
kneading my heaving breast,
while your tongue licks the back of my neck,
as I grind your nature into my hips.

I want you.

My vision
of love during
my days;
the specter
of my desires
during my nights.

I want you.

My delicate,
ebony dream.
Just you.

WE

There once was
a question of you & me
floating in the ether
between the left and right halves
of my brain like a phantom.
And in my mind,
that spectre still haunts
my life like an ill wind.

And the question
at best remains
unanswered;
an empty theory
about the way
we could have been.

I tried to ignore
the question
by rearranging
the memories
in the corners of my mind.

So that all my birthdays
became funerals,
and all the weddings
I attended became nights
I hopped from club to club
trying to drink myself silly,
and fuck the first thing
that came along to forget
about you.

You passed through
my life showering
it with hope and
infinite possibilities
and I
let you slip away.

But the question of us was
still just an empty theory
about the way we could have been.

I was afraid.
You were this shining star
high above me
clothed in mythic proportions
and my own imaginative distortions
and when I found out through
a mutual friend that you were gay . . .

Well, I convinced myself
that it was cool.

Well, damn it,
it wasn't cool.
It wasn't.
I was crushed.
At my wit's end,
I felt abandoned by you.

Well, not necessarily *you.*
Just the *you* I thought that *you* were.
Right. You know.

And shit,
if you only knew the
impossibly convoluted sex
that played out between us
in the midst of my id
and frontal lobe, I swear.

If only you could look
inside my mind and see all
the twisted dreams,
wasted fantasies,
and spoiled jars of body pudding
lying around, well,
you'd know.
You'd really fucking know
and then I wouldn't be
writing this poem and
spitting my guts out
in dark smoke filled rooms
at open mics where hopefully
those who are mutual acquaintances
of ours are not present.

Because I should have known.
I think I should have.
I don't know.
But, on the question of us,
at least I know now
that the answer is no.

That question,
at best, is only an
empty theory about

the way we never were.

THIRSTY

That hefty fellow walked into my bar again last week. He took a seat at the end of the bar on the squeaky stool that every other person who comes here has the good sense to avoid. He looked lonely, and smelled awful. Inwardly, I chuckled at the pathetic sight. I could only imagine what his sob story was going to be. I handed him his usual, and he took a swig. I waited for it, and then he spoke:

"Right now, the deepest parts of me are pulsing with your memory. You beautiful creature, you have captured every part of me. Your way, your whim, your being; everything *you* is what I want.

"I keep trying to think of ways to say this without sounding thirsty. But, fuck it, I am thirsty.

"The reservoir of my passions, my hopes, my dreams: it is all dried up with this constant feverish need to be near you, by your side. Always, caring for you and loving you.

"That's right, I said it. I love you.

"And I know that I don't have much to offer anybody but my time and a broken heart, which houses a broken, overused, spirit. But, they still feel, they still yearn, and they still have the ability to want somebody; to need someone. So that part of me at least works.

"But, these broken parts are housed in this funny shape, this frame--this unknowable persona that many have even ventured to call ugly. And yes, this body has been the star attraction at many a lonesome pity party. It makes noises and funny smells at the most unfortunate times. It doesn't always wear matching socks. The legs are prickled with razor stubble; the feet are eagle talons that stink.

"I could go on.

"But, this thing I am, it still lives. It pains me to go on, but I still live. I live and I love. Or at least I want to. Love.

"I'm so thirsty. My dry lips have waited a lifetime with bated breath for a lover's kiss on a lonely street corner, or a coffee shop, or a bar.

"Tonight, I got a sip when I walked in and said, 'hello'.

"Within this heart of mine, the ground beneath my feet quaked and my world stopped. And for this space, this moment within a split second, there was just us.

"That was a whole half hour ago. Back then.

"However, now, you don't see me. And that parch in the back of my throat is there again. And that's ok, love. That's ok."

I was speechless. He finished the bottle in three loud gulps, slammed the empty thing on the bar, and then stared me right in the eye. I couldn't look away.

"That was beautiful," I said.

"Really," he said. I nodded and licked my lips

seductively.

"You're not my type, honey." He said smirking. "I was talking to the beer. And when you're finished sopping up your spit, I'll have another."

RAGE OF BLACKNESS

Black?
Forget about
just being black.
Blackness is a
state of mind
and your mind can always
change from that.

And mine has changed.
All the way from *yes we can*
back to *they don't really give a fuck about us,*
All of us still fuss,
and cuss, and holler,
just trying to be heard.

Forget about it.
Forget about being black.
Evidently, life isn't about that.
Life was never about our state of mind
especially when it is so cohesively intertwined
with our state of being.

Put simply, who gives a shit?
I do.

I see Black
on the news.
I hear it
shouting in my music.
I see it
in my skin

radiating from
my own reflection.
I read it
in the last words
of Troy Davis before
he was given
that lethal injection.
I heard it
in Trayvon Martin's
screams for help--
that young man
had no chest protection.

And I thought:
This can't be real.
I don't want this
to be my reality.
A country where
reasonable doubt
can still get you killed
while all the real killers
are still running free.

Fuck this.
I just want
to close my eyes
and forget about it.

Forget about:
Over 400 hundred years
of history, struggle, & triumphs
mingling with days of sorrow
and jubilee, because

for all I know and see
in this life, nothing changes.

Forget about it.
Forget about just
being black.

Blackness is only
a state of mind
and that is the only
ever-changing fact.

From slaves in plantation quarters,
to ghetto American public housing;
From 1960s radicals wearing afros,
to mass produced gangster rap heroes;
From the knotty dreds
back to the jehri curl
and every other fad
in between that
had us all screaming
to fit into a
mold of social
and anti-social extremes!
I still say forget it!
Shit!
Forget all about it!

Because they don't really
give a fuck about us!
And they don't have to.
They don't see us, they can't.
When they look at you or me,

they still see an animal.
A thing meant to be subjugated,
whored out for money
or locked in a steel cage.

Black.
Forget about it!
Forget the ideals
of brotherhood and unity
and *can't we all just get along*
for the sake prosperity.
No, we can't.
This system isn't broken,
because it is still life
as usual for you and me.

Forget about it!
Forget what you were told
about us in their history.
Our historical world value
doesn't begin or end
with Civil Rights, and slavery.

So, forget it!
We don't need to evolve.
Our culture, our heritage,
our very existence is revolution.
So turn around, Black,
and look at yourself.
The next phase may start
with you as the solution.

MY REVOLUTION

I want to be there when it comes.
I want to be there during my own revolution--
not sitting on my ass watching television
with chicken hanging from my lips
and watermelon stains on my chest.
Though some of you might expect that shit.

I want to be in that number.
Glowing in undefeated Black
Sweat pouring with confidence
With my life on track.

My day is coming.
And my beauty will be recognized,
Not trivialized but immortalized.
Not disguised, but out
for all the world to realize
that this voice,
this body, this spirit
runs on pure emotion.

And I want to be there when it comes.
I want to be there during my own revolution.
Not waiting for the next man to arrive,
Not sitting on my wiles, full of ignorance and pride

Sometimes I feel like there is
nothing in this world for me.
I feel penalized
not just for being female,
not just for being Black,
but just for being me.

But my day is coming.
A day I will not hide from.
Until that day I choose not to die
But to ride onward and then some.

What other choices have I got?
I have none.

My day is coming.
I can see it on the horizon.
I want to be there when it happens;
I want to be there during my revolution.

COMMON

Alright,
in the interest
of fairness,
I'll be honest.

I have said
and done
ignorant things.
I can get
and have gotten
very ugly with others.
Does that mean
I should fork over
my reality
to your point of view?

We are all clueless.
We all see things
as we want to see them
first before we even
see them as they are.
All the while,
we justify our own
loose morality
on the lack
we see in others.

For example, yesterday,
I saw a cellphone video with
mothers at a preschool graduation
fighting over one cap
and one gown

while their children
screamed in the background.
Young, single, black mothers.
Grown Women.
Where were the fathers?

And of course
I read the online comments:
The usual closet racists
worm their way into
the formless void
of the internet
where they can be
prophetically and pathetically
themselves without pause
or recompense.

I read all
the comments without
offense, until my eyes
fell on one word
from one comment.

One word.
Not nigger,
not ghetto,
not monkey
but one word
in a phrase stating
that these things
among our people
were common.

Common: as in not likely to change.
Common: as in they are doing what is expected of them.
Common: as in they are all animals.
Common: as in normal.

And I thought:
What the hell is so *normal*
about this diseased anarchy
that is festering in our communities,
our country, and indeed our world?

I still live
a war within myself.
Walking a line
between hope and hopelessness
that splits my soul
down the middle
when I see things
like this on my
television or my computer screen
with my skin color,
and my gender
being used against me.

Common.

Jesus, what was all that suffering for?
Rosa do you now wish you had walked home?
Martin, why should we continue?
Malcolm, I am so weak now.
Because I'm guilty.

And I'll admit:
Sometimes
I wish my black
would just fade away
into a shadow of nonexistence,
clear as the ether
and as malleable as water.

Anything, just not this.
Lord no! Not *common*.
Please, I beg of you.
Not that.

Common is ugly.

Common doesn't give
birth to gods
or to kings.

Common is stagnant,
Common is stifling.

Common is the slowest
way to Hell through this
post racial purgatory
called America.

I won't be just *common*.
I won't do it.
I urge you all,
my people, don't do it.

Don't be *common*.

Because,
Common
is death.

THE FINGER

I was working, if you can call standing in the middle of an empty sales floor working. The time flew by like a stream of molasses encased in ice.

Anyway, I noticed that my boss was just a few feet away chatting with a customer, and I decided to try to do something that looked important, like work. So I earnestly began wiping down the glass counters and rearranging the merchandise in the jewelry case. Feeling a renewed sense of purpose, I hardly noticed that I was being watched.

Then, I noticed this little girl. She was just staring at me with so much intention in her little blue eyes. It was as if she wanted to burn a hole through me. She looked like a second grader, tall enough to be a third. I didn't have any kids, so I wouldn't have known.

Anyway, without any warning, her little index finger jutted out in my direction as I said, "May I help you?"

She said nothing back. She just kept giving me the index finger and the death ray stare. So, not to be daunted by a child, I stared back at her and waited for it. But keep in mind I didn't know what it was. For eons of seconds, the world just seemed to drop away, and it was just me, this little white girl and her index finger inching slowly toward my black right arm.

And then it happened. She poked me! Without a single word from her, she poked me and then jumped like she had just received an electric shock. Our eyes met, and I could see that she was afraid of me.

I laughed softly, shook my head, and said, "No, little girl, it never comes off."

She just stared at me, clearly confused and most likely embarrassed. In one quick fluid motion, she turned around and walked toward my boss and the customer who were still chatting away. She didn't even look back at me, as she took her mother's hand. After exchanging further pleasantries with my boss, they soon left the jewelry store.

I never saw that child again, but I would like to think I made an impression on her. She certainly made an impression on me.

THE RULES FOR GOING H.A.M.
(HATERS of ASININE MUSIC)

1st rule of H.A.M.:
Don't get it twisted,
We aren't trying
to destroy hip hop
as we know it
We are trying to save it.

Save it from people,
principalities and powers
that play us against it
and us against each other.

And I am tired.
Aren't you tired?

Tired of being played
by an industry that sells
narcissistic self affirming
schlock to undereducated
masses of Americana,
i.e. our youth,
getting rich while
they suffer to fit
in a mold that was never made
for them to fit in, and
then calling it individuality.

I never knew black face
came in so many shocking colors.
Like pink, and

I thought or I think
that last Friday
it was Euro hyped white skin
and blond hair.
But I digress.

2nd rule of H.A.M.:
Fuck the Illuminati!
Don't get me twisted,
there is obviously
something wrong with
this bullshit
the world is calling rap.
But, are we
passing the buck
or the blame to them
when we say the devil
made them do that?
Shit people; don't be sheeple—
just stop buying their records.

I know it's hard
to think for yourself,
go against the grain
and not go with the flow.
But, could we please have a rapper
with a flow with more Common sense,
who doesn't applaud, get a Grammy
and then thank God for
bitches, bling and violence?

Can we retard
the malignant growth

of stupidity in our community
that self destructively tells
the world that it's ok
if we kill each other daily
because we learned it in a song?

3rd rule of H.A.M.:
Always remember the days
when a rhyme couldn't
get you killed.
Remember the days
we struggled to find
the end of our rainbow,
and when we found it,
we basked in the glow
that was us.
Not the shit they
sell us on TV now,
but the real us.

Remember,
Black is still beautiful
and real Rap is true poetry.
And the truth
was and always is hard to swallow.

Remember these rules
and our battle cry:
Don't Follow Anyone.
Just Go H.A.M.!

MY SOUND

I know who I am
I know what I look like
I can't help how this sounds to you
I am just trying to get in your ear
The same way a beggar
might use your pity and fingers to
get into your wallet.

Give me a moment and let me in.
It won't cost you anything
but you may lose some ignorance
free of charge.

Now, I just have one question:
How black do I sound?
How **'*nigger*'**-ish?
I don't really know.
With my own ears
I can't really hear it.

Am I supposed to say
Po-ah-trey
This way or that?
And when I spit
those verses of mine,
should I have a
back beat with that?

I can't be anything more
or less than myself
And if I sound silly to you
how must I sound to everyone else?

Look, I know a wear my enunciation
proudly on the tip of my tongue.
And I have heard better poets spit tonight
so I know I am not the only one.

If my crotch
had a dick in it
for me to grab onto,
and I had a broad flat chest,
with my pants sagging low
Spitting verses about struggles,
guns and ghettos--
with syllabic inflection
on every word
from my tongue--
would you still see me
as trying to sound so white?
Or rather would you be
more excepting of
my persona
if I was white?

Nah, you hear me.
You feel me.
This is how I sound,
this is my Po-ah-trey.
You don't have to like
what I say, or how it comes out.
But how can you *not* listen,
and still know what I am about?

THE REASON

I started my
Spoken Word journey
in the basement
of The Elks Club
with a faux revolutionary group.

And it was while
I fell for the leader,
and tried to be a cheerleader
for the Black masses
of my community that
I found my voice.

I eventually left
and tried to go out
on my own when I
realized the revolution
revolved around me
playing step and fetch it
to an empty Klan-like
ideology with skin darker than mine.
Wordlessly, I left
in the middle
of a meeting.

Later on,
I would try my hand at open mics
in and out of my community.
This opened my eyes
to all Spoken possibilities,
but I came undone with the idea
of Spoken Word with Unity.

Apparently, they are
mutually exclusive
when you don't
have your own CD
or you can't expound
on the virtues of hip hop
or write poems about sex & booty

Still, I carried on.

I ended up in a club
in Waukegan, IL
that was just a joke.
Full of tried and true,
crusty, phony folk
whose only purpose
was to blow cigar smoke,
get drunk and yell,
Man that poem was dope!
even if they don't hear
or care for a word you say.
Still, for some reason,
the club owner
wanted me around anyway.

I was naïve enough
to believe enough
in a person I had seen on TV
Def Jam dreams were enough
to be a smoke screen for me.
I lost my time,
I lost my mind
and so much money

But the main thing
I lost was my sense
of self and dignity.

My mind was awash with all
the Spoken promises
that were all broken
for the sake of this thing
called poetry.

I did this for Def Jam.
I did this for the Revolution.
I did this shit for the love of people
who were just out to use me.

Well, now, I hate DEF JAM.
And, by the way, fuck the REVOLUTION.
I could give a damn about comedy clubs.
They are full of noise pollution.

But, in the middle of this poetry race,
I have to keep up my own pace.
If I am to become the person
I know I can be
I have to realize
that the only poet
that matters now is me.

And I can't go backwards now.
I have to keep fighting.
My voice,
my poetry,
is the reason

I keep writing.

PLAYING PROMETHEUS

*All right, some of you may agree with this, some may not.
Chances are, all of you will applaud anyway.*

My definition of poetry
is simply words that
bring light to the dead.
You see, there are
too many people
that get this shit twisted
and think that it's cute
to play Prometheus
and like a moth they dangle
wistfully by the flame,
get too close, and are consumed.

Fuck them.
They don't know shit anyway.
They don't realize that poetry
is only worth as much as the poets
think of themselves.
It's that personal.

At the end of the day,
a poet may appreciate his or her audience.
But, when a poet spits a poem,
they shouldn't really give a shit
if you don't like or get it.

Do you think it
takes intelligence to do this?
It doesn't. Not really.
But you applaud them anyway.

For example:
If a poet has ass on the brain 24/7,
he going to write about booty all the time.
He is going to
spit shit that he would
never ever do to any living being.
I guarantee that as the next poet speaks,
no person in the history of the world
is having better sex than what
you are imagining right now
while he spits his fantasy
into your head.
And the joke is you've been mind fucked,
and you still applaud him for it.
Or her.

And then, there are
the pseudo-revolutionary dissidents
among you who may think spoken word
is about community, and power to the people.
And that's really fucking cute.

You sell your books
along with Chinese oils
with African labels,
and want your audience
to believe that you are highly
enlightened and civilized.
You want your audience
to believe that you are
the resurrection of the Last Poets,
Haile Selassie, Bob Marley and

Jesus Christ, themselves.
And that the final 'we shall overcome' solution
is written in every book and CD you sell.

Well, hell, I can find a morsel of nourishment
in a pile of dung if look hard enough can't I?
Look, I can't argue with you
if you already sold the argument
to yourself. I am just saying
it is dangerous to play Prometheus.

There is nothing worse than
when a man or woman's word
contradicts his or her own life.
Frankly, it sucks.
It makes the poet as dead as
the audience they are pretending
to bring light to. And so we have
the dead leading the dead in a circle
that leads to nowhere,
mindlessly sifting through refuse
for tiny morsels of nourishment.

Don't get this shit twisted.
This poem is a warning.
I used to play Prometheus.
I got burnt.
I don't want to play anymore.
I hope you've all learned from my story.

Now you can applaud.

WAITING
(For the children and parents of Newtown, Connecticut)

I wait.
I've been waiting.
Ever since I heard
my first church sermon
at the tender age of five.

"You know," said the preacher,
"These are the last days."

And I thought:
What could this mean?
What are we preparing for?
I have to know.
And I wish some parental figure
in my life had had the sense
that God gave them to know
what I was asking.
See, I wanted to know,
why did we have to die?

From the age of five years,
that little girl
eventually blossomed
into a jaded teenager whose answer
to her five year old self was,
Shit happens, girl I don't know!
because the fear remained.

And I wished my teenaged self
had had the good sense that God

gave her to tell her inner child:
Girl, I don't want to die,
I just don't know
a better way to live.
But I didn't.
I gave that good sense away
because the fear remained.

When I look back over my life,
And I think things over . . .

It seems like
that fear has always
been a factor for me.

So, when I turned on the news last Friday
and heard about twenty
5 to 6-year old kids
dying in school at the
hands of a lone gunman--

I had to look inside of myself
to find and ask
the little girl in me:
Little girl, were those
children anything like you?

And the answer is always the same.
A soft whisper reverberating
in my spirit says, "*We still are.*"
Because the fear remains.

No, I'm not innocent anymore.

And even good little girls and boys can
grow up to become pimps and whores.
No.
What I am still is mortal.
And with that
comes the realization
that I can't fake my way
out of death
with the machinations
of my childhood imagination,
and I can't turn off
the horrors that I see
in front of me
by flicking a switch
to watch cartoons,
sleeping in mommy's bed
or just eating my cereal.

So,
what can I do?
What have I become?
Someone please tell me,
so I can look inside and
tell that scared little girl
in me what happens
to us when we die!
But, you don't know.
Hell, I still don't know.
So, I wait.
And I'm still waiting.

**When I look back over my life,
and I think things over . . .**

A MOTHER'S HANDS

Not much to look at.
Not too big or small.
Not well kept or manicured.
Sometimes the skin is chapped raw.
The palms of them are calloused over.
Dirt is clouding their fingertips.
But, they still exist.
These hands, a mother's hands,
live to feel, to create, to be.

Capable of great things are these hands.
Reaching for things you couldn't
or wouldn't touch with yours.

With these hands,
I will nurture the generations
who will lead the revolts of our future.
I will feed them, I will clothe them;
I will hold them when they are scared;
heal them when they hurt.

I will sacrifice with these hands.
And as long as blood beats through them,
they are stronger than you will ever know.

THANK GOD FOR WHO I AM NOT

You know
I like being
who I am.
Today anyway.
And I thank God
for who I am not.

I am not a lemming:
a small rodent,
easily lead by her friends,
and her libido.
I can think for myself.
I can just as easily walk
away from the cliff
as run to it.
Besides, I am
afraid of falling.

I am not a dog:
Though I do wish
I had a tail
so that others
could see how I felt
without me having to tell them,
I would just as soon not
sniff the posterior of others
as a formal greeting.
I would be a lonely dog.

I am not
Queen of a bee colony.
I do not want to spend

my whole day in one room
getting humped by random drones
and laying thousands
of nameless bastard eggs.
With wings, I would like to think
I would have better things to do.
Like flying.

So what am I?
I am a fully autonomous writer
of the female persuasion
with no husband,
no kids,
and no tail.
Thank you, God!

But, I really wish
I had that tail.

DOWN

I've been so down
even time wrote me off,
handing me over to circumstances
beyond my control.
But I am not
crying about it.
No, I am not.

These tears you see
in my eyes now
are not for
missed opportunities
or wasted time;
social discrepancies
or the unethical mishap
of falling in love.

These tears are not
for my enemies
or fair weather acquaintances
who wrote me off with time,
foolish in thinking
their disfavors
were enough to silence me.

These tears are not even
for want of your affections,
your attentions,
or your slavish admirations.
For that, I will buy a dog.

No, these tears are for me.

Because I am still here.
My blood still pumps
and my ink still bleeds.
And I can hear
the thunderous adulations
of my own heart.

REFLECTING IN THE LIGHT OF MO'BETTA BLUES

Tonight
I'm feeling Bleek;
My blues is Mo Betta
laying alone,
half naked,
half heartedly listening
to an uncensored story
on my television screen;
writhing in my sheets
while writing this poem
from nonexistence.

Reflecting that
I have never been
a poetic trendsetter.
Tonight won't be any betta'.
Tonight, I lay alone,
lonely in sin with
a deliciously wicked grin
on my lips;
my pen scratching on paper;
my sweat running out
of my skin in huge drips.

Ba do dwee, Ba do da, Ba do da.

I guess I let Mr. Lee,
spike my mental potion again like:

Ba do dwee, Ba do da, Ba do da.

As Bleek's horn testifies

in my ear, my back is to
the storied motions on screen
and my nose is to my paper.
My time edified,
watching the movie in my mind
like I think I've dreamed
these scenes before.

Reflecting on the real.
Me.
I am a little like Bleek.
Artistic, selfish and sensitive.
Safe in my head though,
cause I can't hang
in the real world so
I grab a pen
and reorder my own vision
with words on an empty page.

Ba Do Dwee, Ba Do Da . . .

In my dreams
Light becomes dark,
like a Shadow creeping
his black fingers up
the small of my back,
my hand grips my pen tighter
with it's tip against the paper,
scratch, scratch, scratch

Ba do Dwee, Ba do da, ba do da

Too bad,

I don't have
an Indigo man
or a Clark Boy
to share my Bleek,
and Shadow dreams with yet.
Or so I reflect.

Just biding my time,
Just biding my time.

Ba do Dwee, Ba do da, Ba do da

Until my body finds sleep,
I write—
with Mo' Betta' Blues
on my mind tonight.
Just Mo' Betta Blues
on my mind tonight.

THE BLUES FALLS LIKE RAIN FOR ME

Sometimes
I listen to the rain
as it falls outside my window.
Each drop makes it's own individual sound
like drums beaten to the rhythm of my soul.
The rain sings to me.

The rain sings the blues in my heart,
and my spirit swims through the voices of Muddy Waters,
John Coltrane, uninhibited, unashamed and clean.

I imagine myself as the star attraction
in a juke joint on the Mississippi Delta
dancing alone in a room filled with couples in motion.
As the roof leaks and the floors creak, I dance.

I feel the raindrops in my eyes,
dropping in buckets, as my cotton sun dress
clings to my hips, and my thighs,
while I smile and turn and wind my emotions around me.

I imagine a dark man with
hand and face weathered by time
strumming a guitar with his fingertips
and as the rain falls around me,
from the stage his words single me out and caress me.

I hear his words as he sings to me
much like I hear the raindrops.
His words are slow.
He says to me: *If you are going to walk all over my love
woman, the least you can do is take off your shoes.*

And I laugh, and kick my heels up high,
and my shoes come flying off.

He doesn't even smile back at me.
He is so cool. He just keeps playing
and singing my sadness away.

And he keeps singing to me while I dance.
And I dance alone for him and the rain.

WHEN TAALAM KISSED THE APPLES OF MY CHEEKS

His lips were soft, silky.
Shadow dark, like ripe plums.
And they felt like a wish;
sweet, childlike, and innocent.

My face flushed with blood.
My mind awash with shock.

And me, looking up
into his intelligent eyes,
with dry mouth and lips--

said simply, *Hello. Nice to meet you, Taalam.*

And I meant it.

EPILOGUE

As the pages of my life continue to turn on, it is time for me to stop and reflect. I have many people to thank for this book, but first I have to thank God the Father and The Son, my Savior, Jesus Christ. I know that I have sworn and used vulgarities in this book. I can and will acknowledge my own faults. However, like I said in the first book, if I told anyone I would never swear again (on page or on stage), I know I would be lying and He would too. So, I must say thank you to HIM for allowing me to yet live, and to give me time to say thank you to HIM for blessing me with the gift of free expression.

Please note, when I write poetry, or anything for that matter, I am trying to make sense of the world I live in and myself. So, a lot of these poems are reactions and observations on things I've seen or done. If you see yourself in anything I write, then you have written yourself into the story that is my life. Congratulations, you're in there. I have been through many ups and downs for the sake of poetry or whatever the fuck I thought I was doing for poetry. I am still getting over many a hurt and betrayal.

This journey has been a lonely uphill climb. And I am tired of feeling sorry for myself. There is something I will admit here that I was not ready to admit in the last book. I have bipolar mania, and I have been suffering with it for a long time. I learned this about myself while I was writing the first book. It doesn't change what happened to me, but acknowledging this helps me understand my part in the things that led to the writing of "Random Acts of Verse".

I had things twisted big time. I knew it took courage to get up there and spit a hastily written poem the first few times. You mostly get a pass when people haven't heard you before. Well, usually you do. No one seems to know how to respect the microphone anymore unless you look or sound a certain part.

That said, there is a reason I call myself a "performance poet" and not a "spoken word artist". My palette is me. If you see or hear anything in me that is relatable while listening to me, then I have done my job.

Part of performance poetry is telling your own truth. And, in the end, all I am selling is my own self. This is dangerous when coupled with Spoken Word. Spoken word artists are activists. They push their words out to evoke change in their immediate world.

I can't be a spoken word artist. I won't lead the revolution. I'm still healing. I can't lead anyone to the Promised Land while I am still trying to dig myself out of the last ditch I fell into. The best way to lead is by example. I am not the best poet out there, but I do believe that I am getting better. The poems "Playing Prometheus" & "The Reason" best depict why I can't be a spoken word artist. I have known too many revolutionary hypocrites in my time, but I don't want to become one of them.

Life and death are on the tongue. You enter that slam or open mic and you grip that microphone at your own risk. But, first, do it for yourself. Write what you feel and experience with your own senses. And don't try to live vicariously through false idols and lost prophets. That is free advice from someone who lost her way while playing with words.

The last five poems of this book were fun to write and fun to perform. One of them, "Thank God for Who I am not," was recently published in Chicagopoetry.com's journal of Modern Poetry (The 14th edition of Chicago's Poetry Cram Series). I consider CJ Laity to be a friend of mine and ChicagoPoetry.com has been a valuable asset to the Chicago Poetry scene. The last poem, however, is special.

True story, I was in Milwaukee, WI. I had just gotten off the stage after bombing terribly, and I was being ridiculed by the same poets who had invited me up there numerous times before. I was ready to give up.

Well, I got my first lifeline in the form of a kiss on the forehead and some words of advice from one of the greatest poets in the known world: Taalam Acey.

He said, "Your poetry should only matter to one person first. And that is you."

Of course, I am paraphrasing now. I was shocked that he would even deem me worthy of a second glance, let alone a pep talk. So, his kind words sort of washed over me.

I have to thank my mother, Sally Harris, for believing that I could do anything if I put my mind to it. I would like to thank all the artists of North Chicago, Illinois for letting me into their lives. Believe it or not, I have learned a lot from all of you.

Check me out on www.twitter.com/PoeticHarris and look for my CD "My Time: The Words of Jacqueline Nicole Harris".

www.cdbaby.com/jacquelinenicoleharrisan

A special thank you goes to Marques "DJ Skillz" Smith-Walker for designing the cover of this book. I couldn't have done a better job in my wildest dreams. And I will be forever grateful.

But not his kindness. His kindness was like a rock. And I've been building on that stone ever since.

AUTHOR'S NOTES

As a child and a young adult, the blues was alive and well every weekend at our house. My mother grew up on it; she loved it. And I grew to respect it.

Several artists in my mother's record and tape collection stood out. Two in particular were Bobby Blue Bland and B. B. King.

Bobby Blue Bland's song "Take off Your Shoes" was released on his **Midnight Run** album by Malaco Records on July 19, 1989. I was twelve years old. It was probably one of the most hardcore songs about a guy in love getting cheated on I had ever heard. And I couldn't end this book without acknowledging the legend that he was.

The song "Take off Your Shoes" was written by Frederick Knight and Bettye Crutcher. Bobby Blue Bland, sadly enough, passed away on June 23, 2013, and I dedicate the poem "The Blues Falls Like Rain For Me" to him. It is his voice I imagine every time I speak that poem though I never heard him play guitar.

Thank you for being a part of my life, Mr. Bland.

71

Made in the USA
Charleston, SC
07 November 2013